Photo: DaSean Lee

How To Grow Up Like Me

The Ballou Story Project

Created by the writers of Ballou Senior High School
in collaboration with Shootback and Shout Mouse Press

Published by
Shout Mouse Press, Inc.
www.shoutmousepress.org

Copyright © 2014 Shout Mouse Press, Inc.

ISBN-13: 978-0692309568 (Shout Mouse Press, Inc.)
ISBN-10: 069230956X

All photography produced in partnership with Shootback Project
Cover photograph by DaSean Lee
Interior photographs:
Nina Kitt (p. 58), DaSean Lee (p. i, 12, 20, 31, 38, 41, 44, 63), Randy
Sams (p. 9, 49, 55), Litzi Valdivia-Cazzol (p. iv, 15, 23, 52), DaeDae
Walker (p. 26)

This book is dedicated to those
who have not gotten one about them,
but who deserve it.

Contents

Prologue

I learned that courage was not the absence of fear,
but the triumph over it.
The brave man is not he who does not feel afraid,
but he who conquers that fear.

-- Nelson Mandela

Photo: DaSean Lee

We are more
than where we came from.
We are more
than what others imagine us to be.

Prologue

For a group of eleven dedicated Ballou High School freshman, it started with an exercise: Write a set of instructions for "How to Grow Up Like Me." Use the major events of your life. Give advice. Tell stories. Create moments that come alive.

For six ambitious seniors, it started with a call to action: Your story is your strength. Show me—show the college admissions and scholarship folks, show the kids like you who need inspiration when it gets tough—how you became such survivors and successes.

I challenged both groups, above all else, to be real. Be yourself, and be brave. Honesty and vulnerability take courage, and acts of courage inspire change. You have a tremendous opportunity here to change the hearts and minds of your readers: both to think of you differently, and to dream differently of our own potential and promise.

I could not have imagined how fearlessly, how generously, and how beautifully these writers would face this challenge, head-on. Nor how seriously they would take their responsibility to serve as a beacon for those who need it most.

Some writers used the exercise to find specific life stories they wanted to explore. Others kept the idea of the instruction manual. Every writer told a story that needed to be told.

Within this book you will find stories of everyday challenges of growing up: riding the bus on your own, learning to play an instrument, overcoming shyness, facing defeat on the field. These writers know that small daily decisions add up to your life and your character; every step is a step either towards or away from who you want to be.

You will also find stories of burdens no young adult should have to bear: loss of parents, loss of homes, physical and emotional violence between those who are supposed to love each other most. These are the thundering forces that can shape a person's life, but these writers refuse to let these challenges define them. They make clear through their words and their spirit: We are more than where we came from. We are more than what others imagine us to be.

We used a combination of writing techniques to compile these stories. Sometimes writers wrote, and sometimes they dictated. We wanted to blur the line between writing and story-telling, to show that writing is as much about shaping and editing as it is about generating words. And, most importantly, we wanted to capture authentic voices on the page. So often in writing we worry that what we have to say isn't enough, so we try to make it sound complicated and important. We write "the consequences of my actions resulted in a significant transformation" when what we mean is: "I changed." We learned that if you are honest and vulnerable and real, as these courageous writers are in this book, what you have to say is enough. It is more than enough. Read these powerful essays and you'll see.

I was humbled and moved by so many aspects of this project, and by every one of these writers. Perhaps most striking was the selflessness, the willingness of these writers to share—first with me and then with a reading public—not only their hopes but also their heartaches. Raw, exposed, and bare. They do so in the hopes that it will help others in similar situations to know they are not alone.

I was also struck by the determination of these writers to create their own center of gravity, often against backdrops of constant change: switching homes, switching schools, switching families, readjusting. These writers develop the strength to be their own rock. "Find yourself," one author writes, "because you can't understand anything if you don't understand yourself." Another says, powerfully: "In the meantime, I love myself for everyone who doesn't."

This is why we write. The stories we tell about ourselves make all the difference. All too often the narrative of these writers' lives is told by outsiders, emphasizing their unfortunate proximity to violence. That's not the only story. We are who we tell ourselves we are, including who we've been, and who we can become. In writing *How to Grow Up Like Me*, these authors have taken control of their own narratives. They make their stories their strength. They write leaning forward, with ambition and purpose, re-imagining each next page.

-- Kathy Crutcher, May 2014

Photo:
Litzi Valdivia-Ca

I just call them
temporary forevers.

How To Grow Up Like Me
by M.H. Jordan

1. Be born. Be born struggling.

After I was six weeks old, I was constantly going back to the hospital. I had ear infections that made me scream so loud I could barely sleep. I couldn't do anything but cry.

I had tubes placed in my ears that repeatedly fell out. The doctor told them that if the tubes kept falling out then I might become deaf. We waited. They watched. I listened.

And now, even though it's still hard, I can hear.

2. Be curious. Be careful.

At two years old, I was crawling around while my mother was on the phone. Being the mischievous child that I was, I decided to go to a socket with a bobby pin in-hand and put it in there.

The result of my actions was a delayed cry for help.

I felt it immediately when it happened but I couldn't express my emotions just as fast. Because of that, my mother had no idea that I was being electrocuted, and I couldn't just come out and tell her because I didn't know what was going on myself.

By the time sound finally escaped my mouth, it was too late. The damage had already been done.

3. Be smart. Be responsible.

At first starting school was the easiest thing for me, but because I was used to being with my mother and family all the time, it made the process even harder. That thought in my head was of being so far away and alone. Eventually I coped with not being able to be like other kids, because I wasn't.

That was also my first time having to be the only one in my neighborhood or family to do something responsible. Throughout my whole life I've had to do everything a step earlier than everyone else. This was just the beginning of my adult childhood.

4. Be scared. Be brave.

Elementary school went by fast. I won a spelling bee, I was in TAG, this program for advanced students. That was hard because I was dyslexic and everybody told me I would get kicked out. But I stayed, and when I left, I was in the top five in the class. I tried hard. I didn't want to fail my family. I didn't want to fail myself.

One memory stands out: I was nine, and I was walking home off the school bus. There was a dark alley I had to walk past, and I didn't want to walk past alone. A man jumped out. He had a stick, and he tried to hit me with it. He grabbed me, but I ran. I cried and ran and breathed heavy and ran. All I could hope was that he was not behind me.

For a long time I wouldn't go outside. I wouldn't talk to anybody.

But I couldn't live in fear. That was the first time I had to get over something serious.

5. Be mad. Be stubborn.

The first day of seventh grade, I was excited and eager to be starting my second year in middle school: wearing new uniforms, being looked up to and not looked down on. And yes, this was only seventh grade. As I was getting ready for school, though, I had this aching in my stomach that something bad would happen. I ignored it at first but then it got a little more painful. I told my mother and she said that I was just nervous and thinking about it too much. It was only my imagination and constant over-thinking of things, nothing too serious.

As I was almost finished getting ready, it happened. We got a loud banging on our door. It was the police. All the sheriffs were coming into our apartment, raiding us, and waking up the babies. One sheriff came into the bathroom where I was and pointed his gun in my face. My first thought was to throw my hands up and do as I was told but he started cursing at me and putting his hands on me and I refused to do what he said until he took a better tone with me and got his hands off of me. In the back of my mind I still had thoughts like, *What if I get locked up for disobeying him?* and *What if his gun accidentally goes off by him bumping into the door frame?*

Finally I went with my instincts and went into the living room. As I walked out I heard my mother crying. My stepfather was making groaning noises and painful faces as they put the handcuffs on him. I just sat there silently for a minute and a tear ran down my face. A million and one thoughts came rushing to my mind but I ignored them and just sat there quietly. I didn't answer any questions. I wouldn't tell them what school I went to, what my name was, or how old I was. It pissed them off but they didn't say anything because they could tell this was a bad experience for me.

After a few more minutes I just got up and finished getting ready. I gathered my things for school, put on my shoes and coat and left without saying a thing to anyone. As I waited at the bus stop with the other kids they all looked at me weird and asked me questions but all I could think was, *What a great way to start off seventh grade.*

6. Be fatherless. Be hurt.

Everyone tells me constantly that I look just like my father. He's very tall, light skin, once was slim. He had dreads and only wore his goatee. Now he has a beer gut and a haircut to go with his facial hair. He is the most country person you could meet. His South Carolina accent is still strong even though he hasn't been there in years. He has no cut cards—if you ask him something, he'll tell you, no sugarcoating, nothing. He has a bad temper, too, but at the same time he can be loving, caring, respectful, and over-protective.

Unfortunately he wasn't ready to be responsible.

My father left when I was six or seven. He would jump in and out of my life like it was nothing. Like it didn't hurt me in any way. I probably made it seem that way to a lot of people whenever he came up into the subject. But it did hurt, like he just repeatedly reached into my chest and took a piece of my happiness and love with him. Every time he came back, he never brought it back with him. Eventually I became accustomed to this routine and even though it wasn't OK, I sat there with my fake smile and tried my hardest to fight back tears. I bit my tongue so nothing I said would wind up hurting me more. I refused to give that type of power to someone who kept constantly hurting me. I didn't like being vulnerable. It just hurt me in the end.

When he finally left, he didn't come back until I was thirteen, and even then, only for a couple weeks. My mother treated me like I was the reason. Until this day she resents me but tries not to show it. When we talk about it, I can't help but cry because I just know she blames me for it. Even though deep down, I'm hoping she doesn't.

My father always makes false promises. He always says something came up.

I have dreams of what it would be like if he was here. I just call them temporary forevers. Everybody goes through something eventually.

7. Be mature. Move on.

I've left middle school and now I am starting high school. New house, new school, new friends, new environment, new problems, new opportunities, new obstacles. Me and my father are talking again but I haven't seen him since that time when I was thirteen. I'm fourteen now. He has skin cancer and is trying to get his life together before he goes. My mother and I are drifting farther apart. She takes sides with her new boyfriend. She ignores problems. She takes things out on me. She is sick, too, but it's not life or death.

I keep having dreams about the future. They keep coming true. I'm scared of what they're saying. At first I didn't want to tell anybody. But now I'm telling you. When I hold stuff in, it hurts.

I can't just sit there in the moment and be sad. I've got to get over it. When it actually does happen then that's lost time that I can't get back.

5

Now I know I have to take the first step before anyone else can. I want to get an education. I want to do something I know my father would be proud of. I want to accomplish something for myself and have something to look forward to.

I've tried my hardest to find someone to love me, but I haven't found it. Yet. But I'm still looking. And in the meantime, I love

M. H. Jordan

I grew up in Maryland and DC and have six siblings. I like to read and to write poetry and mini-stories. My favorite author is Nina Simone. I hope to become a photographer and journalist and go to Howard. When I was writing this piece, I had to think about the most important things even though I've been through a lot.

Finding a Home
by Carl Brown

When I was really young, we lived in a shelter for about a year. My mother and my grandmother used to argue a lot about things I couldn't understand and my grandmother kicked my mother out. So we moved to the shelter. There were four of us: me, my two older brothers, and my mother. I didn't really know what was going on but I didn't think that this was like a weird or unordinary thing. I was young at the time. Ma said that we were going to be there for just a little while but we ended up living there for six months. When I finally realized what living in a shelter is, I felt surprised to find out that I didn't have a home.

The shelter was made of different dorms. There were different rooms for different groups of people, but we were all mixed together: old, young, men, women, tall, short.

While we were living in the shelter, my mother used to go out a lot and we would have a babysitter watch us. While my mom was going out we would have lots of fun and go places like the movies or parks, and we would always get treats as well. While we were living in the shelter we had to attend daycare. It was just like a classroom but with toys and a big TV. We learned things and had fun in daycare. When we wanted to eat we would have to wait until it was time. The cafeteria was just like a school's cafeteria. The shelter was very friendly and I made lots of friends and memories. We even had a fire and had to evacuate just like we do in school.

When we moved I was pretty sad because I would miss the friends and memories I made there. It had become my home in a way, but there wasn't enough privacy, and not enough space. We wanted a place where we could live on our own rules. We wanted freedom.

My home life had been different before the shelter. At first I lived with my father. While I was living with him we had a pretty good life and a loving family. My father was a good father. He took us to the movies and to restaurants and we had fun. We'd ride bikes, play games, and just hang out. At first my father and my mother were loving and had a good relationship, but then as the years went by, they started arguing. The arguments gradually ended up with us leaving my father.

When we moved away from my dad I was upset. I really didn't know what was going on. I thought that we were just taking a vacation or something. The day after that, I saw my mother, she was crying. I asked her what was wrong. She said, "Nothing," because at the time I wouldn't understand. I asked what was going on and why hadn't Dad come with us. She said, "We are taking a break from Dad for a while and we won't be seeing him any time soon." I was heartbroken to hear that I wouldn't be seeing my dad for a while.

After the first week I started to miss my father and the things we used to do. Even my brothers missed him. I tried to do the things that I did with my father with my mom but it only made me feel worse about Dad not being here. One day my mom noticed something was wrong with me and she said, "What's wrong?" and I said, "I miss my dad." She looked sad but she said, "It will be OK, don't worry." That made me feel better, but only imagine

Photo: Randy Sans

I've been through a lot of struggles.

But I'm still sane and smart
and getting educated
and staying in school.

temporarily. The emptiness comes back after a while. The longing.

Now I've been living in the same place for eight years and it's been pretty stable. I share a room with my brother, but it's close enough to being private. We have space. We have a nice comfortable bed. We have a TV, and cool air, and food on the table. We have family, connection, love, relaxation. We have that freedom we'd been searching for.

I've been through a lot of struggles. But I'm still sane and smart and getting educated and staying in school. My father comes and visits more often and he is about to move back in with us. So things are getting better. I'm happy that he's coming back, so that empty spot can be filled. I'm looking forward to a better home, to a good life.

Carl Brown

I was born in 1998, on December 13. I am from SE Washington, DC. I am 15 years old and am currently attending Ballou High School in the ninth grade. My hobbies are sports, games, cooking, and learning.

Make a Difference

by Essence Milling

There's no single event that made me an adult. It's not "once upon a time I was kid, and then I was a teen and learned how to grow up." For me I skipped that step. I was a kid and then I wasn't.

Since I was 11 years old, I been taking care of myself. My whole life I haven't had a father, and my mother has been in my life only as she wants. When she was around, she sometimes beat me, and I got treated like a stranger by my brothers and sisters. I moved a lot and I've changed from elementary to elementary school, back to back from place to place. I lost both of my grandmothers in the same year. I was abused by a stranger. The list of challenges goes on. And through it all, I had to find a way on my own to get to school, do my laundry, and buy my clothes, shoes, female products, etc. Through it all, I was alone.

I'm about to be 18. It hasn't gotten easier, but it's there. I have learned how not to depend on anyone but myself. I have to be responsible, to look at things from a different perspective. I can't be childish. It's very stressful because you're not prepared for it, and it's hard to go through on your own. So far my plan has been turning out to be ok, but I know at some point there will be a setback. Now that I have my school behind me I know I will make it through all the hard times.

My dream for the future is to make a change in my life and

Photo: DaSean Lee

There's no single event that made me an adult.

I was a kid and then I wasn't.

community. College will help me pursue those dreams. College will not only bring me connections but also it will bring me opportunities to show others what it takes to become a better person than people you might normally see. I have big ideas for this. For example, since I was five years old, I have wanted to own my own business. Specifically, I have wanted to create a business that helps others, that gives them a way to succeed in life. I want to build a business that combines all the major services that people need. Part would be a restaurant, where people could both eat and train to become cooks. Another part would be a salon, where people could find a way to present themselves well and feel good about themselves. There would be a community center, where kids could do their homework and get help with problems at home. Lastly, there would be a job center, where people could learn how to find a job.

This is the kind of place that would have been helpful for me growing up. I want to create an environment where people can get their needs addressed and can be inspired. I want to build a strong community so that people won't always have to fend for themselves. I want to not only follow, but lead for my community. This also means to me that I would be able to do what I always dreamed—to give back to my community and my family—just for the fact that God created me to make a difference.

Essence Milling

I grew up in Maryland and DC. I like all types of music and I play clarinet. My favorite artist is Mary J. Blige. I plan to get my license for cosmetology. This piece was difficult to write but I keep diaries and I like to write about my life.

My Definition of Success
by Allen Weaver

I grew up in Southeast DC, where violence is a big issue. I hear gunshots at night, and sometimes even during the day. I have to be cautious of where I go and I wonder what would happen if I go to the wrong place at the wrong time. Should I go to the store at night? Or should I just wait until the morning? Where I'm from, you've got to be wise. You've got to think outside the box and be one step ahead. You can't show that you're weak, but at the same time you can't be cocky. You have to respect the danger that goes on around you. You have to respect that even kids and teens can get their hands on guns. You have to respect everyone because any sign of disrespect can cause you to lose your life.

Because I've grown up in this environment, I want to be surrounded by people who have different approaches to life. I know that one of the strong suits of going to college is diversity. It's a great place to meet new people from all over the world that you never thought you would without even having to travel. My mindset could be different from that of someone from somewhere else in the world, but I want to experience that difference. I want to understand how other people heal themselves, how they get through tough situations, and what's their definition of success.

My definition of success is to stay positive, to not doubt that I can do something. To do that, I have to be open and curious about the world. That's why I love creativity—it's not the normal way to do something. I want to do more things that are creative,

Photo: Litzi Valdivia-Cazzol

I have to be open and curious
about the world.

like learn how to be an entrepreneur. To learn how to get in people's minds and understand what they like and why. I don't just look at things blindly or go in not knowing, I think deeply about things and how they work. I always want to know what to do and how to do it. I want to learn the correct way but also the wrong way because it shows me what to avoid. I don't want to stop myself from being successful. I bring this curiosity and openness and energy to campus. I show that I'm determined to be one step ahead in life.

Allen Weaver

I grew up in SE Washington, DC and am a senior at Ballou High School. I play football and hope to play professionally one day.

Someone to Believe in Me

by Aijah Roberts

I may be on the college track now, but I haven't always worked so hard in school.

In elementary school I was easily distracted. If we were working and someone tapped a pencil on a desk I would look up. If someone walked through the door I would look up. It was hard to focus when there was a lot of noise. It made me frustrated because I wanted to learn, but at the same time, I couldn't. My teachers would tell my mother that I was a smart and good kid but was easily distracted. At first she wasn't mad, just curious. She wanted to know what it was that was causing me not to stay focused. But later, she thought it was just me, that I was doing it on purpose. That made me feel bad, because she didn't believe me.

In middle school my grades were bad because I still didn't focus. I thought school was pointless. I rushed through my tests and just marked anything. Part of this was from me being distracted and part from me not caring. For a brief time during my 7th grade year things got better, because I moved with my father and started attending a Maryland school where I had lots of help. I liked the school rules and I was able to focus. I tried strategies such as ignoring and gluing my eyes to my paper so I couldn't look up. Most of the time my head was down as I tested so I could not see any thing but my work, and I did better.

But my 8th grade year I had to come back to DC to live with my mom, and I went back to my old school, Johnson Middle School, where my parents met. The kids there were a lot different than in Maryland. In Maryland there were different races. The kids there never walked out of class or there were rarely fights. But back at Johnson kids used profanity a lot and walked out of class or talked back to teachers. Kids acted out.

I did my work and got things done but never turned the assignments in. I began to feel that school was irrelevant. This led to me not trying my best on the DC-CAS and other big tests. I thought the DC-CAS was just for the school but it had my name on it. It was only later that I learned that the scores of my tests were really showing how I was learning and whether I should pass.

My report cards were bad that year. I was nervous about passing to the 9th grade. I talked to my teachers and my administrator about helping me move to the next grade and they told me not to worry, that I was going to pass. I think it was because I was a good student and I never had problems or got suspended. They probably saw that I was mature enough to go to the next grade. I was smart enough, but my grades just weren't showing it. I tried my best at the last moment, the end of the year, and my administrators congratulated me when I made good scores on my tests. I was so happy to graduate and be able to attend high school with my cousins.

But after summer it was school time again and I couldn't go to the school I wanted. I found out I had to go to Ballou High School. I automatically thought I was going to fail because of the things I heard about Ballou. I heard that people were 21 years old and still in high school and that there's always shootings happening. I thought Ballou had no good teachers and related a lot to the movie 'Freedom Writers' because of the neighborhood violence. I didn't want to go there.

When I first got to Ballou, though, it wasn't as bad as I expected. Kids were going to class on time and there were teachers. I expected no teachers, no work, and students in hallways.

I also heard about AVID. AVID is Achievement Via Individual Determination. It's a college prep program. I was told that I was hand-picked to be in this class, and that felt good. I know other people had a chance but they weren't picked. So when I went to my first day of AVID, I went prepared and didn't know what to expect.

When you walk into an AVID class, it's just like any other classroom. The kids are the same, the rules are the same, but something is different. The teacher.

When I first met Ms. Erazo she seemed nice. I never thought she was a teacher who would be so helpful. When you're having a bad day, she will try to cheer you up or make you smile when you don't want to. There's always a bond with her, like having a laugh once in a while or just getting along well.

My teachers in school before were different from Ms. Erazo. Ms. Erazo is the teacher who always pushes you forward and always makes sure you are fine, even when you are struggling. It doesn't matter who you are. You could be the kid that talks a lot or just doesn't do your work and she would still help you. If you're blue or green, if your hair is long or short, she still helps you.

Photo: DaSean Lee

Everybody needs someone
who believes in them.
When someone believes in you,
they motivate you.
They don't give up.
And neither do you.

I like the fact that Ms. Erazo pushes me forward. My previous teachers pushed me, but not the way Ms. Erazo does. Some teachers will let you fall and not help you pick back up. But Ms. Erazo just isn't one of those teachers. Even if I have my head down, she asks if I'm OK, or do I need to talk. Previous teachers just told me to put my head up. One teacher is trying to be there for me. The other is just telling me to get my work done. The first way is motivating because I know that somebody cares.

I have family that pushes me forward at home but Ms. Erazo is like family at school. She has changed me a lot and has done so many good things for me. She tells me I can do stuff, and doesn't let me quit. It's important to have a teacher like Ms. Erazo because everybody needs someone who believes in them. When someone believes in you, they motivate you. They don't give up. And neither do you.

Aijah Roberts

I was born in Washington, DC. I attend Ballou Senior High School. I draw and dance for fun. I'm in the 9th grade and I graduate in 2017. I still don't like to work hard, but Ms. Erazo and AVID made me realize how important it was. I thought about getting out of AVID before but I'm glad I didn't because I wouldn't have gotten to share my story with the Ballou Story Project.

Overcoming Failure
by Tarrance Brooks

I'm not proud to admit this, but during the most important game of the football season, I gave up.

We were in the playoffs and the weather was deadly. It was cold, rainy, and just a little bit of light shone onto the field. As soon as we stepped onto the field I felt defeat. The feeling was strange because in previous games I was pumped, jumping around with lots of energy. But this time we were not prepared. We thought the game would be postponed and we were upset we had to play. None of us were dressed appropriate. Our coach had to get extra socks and cut them to provide an arm sleeve. I felt a little embarrassed but most people didn't know the arm sleeve was a sock. Some of the players on my team said, "This is dumb. We will be laughed at." I replied, "Come on guys, we have to stick with it." But the way I said it was with a dry and low tone because I didn't want to play, either. It was too cold.

We got off to a bad start. My team was used to me being ready to play, but since I wasn't encouraging enough, they felt doubt. I started to jump to get warmed up, but in my head I was not ready. My mother and father were in the crowd, and they knew just by the look on my face something was wrong. My mother shouted, "Get it together, Tarrence!" We took our place on the bleachers. It felt as if the weather was teasing us because as time went by, the wind grew stronger and stronger.

Photo: Litzi Valdivia-Cazzol

Now the challenges motivate me.
I'll try to overcome.

The game began. The quarterback for our team couldn't catch the snap because his hands were frozen. Our running back, my brother, was too cold to run so he sat down and gave up. Some of the other players also came and just sat down. I was emotional. I knew the game was lost now but we had to finish. I couldn't tackle or anything because I just kept focusing on the cold and not thinking about the game. The other team was playing like it wasn't cold, like it was the summer. They were running the ball fast and just jumping up and acting excited.

Towards the end of the game, the score was 0-0. The running back for the other team ran down the field and scored the game-winning touchdown. As he ran down the field, no one attempted to catch him. We just let him score.

We felt defeat. We gave up on ourselves and our fans. People were disappointed, but after the game they cheered us on anyway, yelling, "Let's go Buccaneers!" They wanted us to hold our heads up and learn from this lesson and keep moving forward.

Our coach gathered us together and he started off like this: "We played hard out there." Then he asked a rhetorical question. He said, "Do you guys think you gave it your all?" I knew he was talking about me, trying to give clues that I let him down.

When he dismissed us he brought me to the side. He started telling me how I didn't play as I usually did and how things may have been different if I did play harder. I looked discouraged so he said, "Look, this is a good experience for you, so now you will know how to handle situations like this in the future." Every time he told me something I tried not to walk away and let it go in one ear and out the other. I took in his advice. His teaching was encouraging and that made me want to become great. I knew I was great, but he wanted me—and I wanted myself as well—to become greater. He said to me, "You're a leader on and off the field." Then he gave me a big pat on the back and sent me on my way.

This was a time I will never forget. This is a time I came across failure because I put myself before my team. In other situations like these I now know how to handle them and come with a better attitude. This is why I put so much effort in my schoolwork, activities, and other things because I do not want to experience this failure again. The lesson I took from this is to work hard and never give up, always stay strong. Sometimes in school, during an exam or anything that takes hard work and lots of thinking, I'm faced with challenges. But now the challenges motivate me. I'll try to overcome. Most people who are successful had to overcome a lot of challenges, and it inspires me to do the same as they did.

I see myself as an inspiring leader for kids my age. Having role models helps kids stay off the street and not to wind up locked up or killed. It helps them become the next Einstein, Martin Luther King, or however they see themselves in the future. It helps them focus more and strive for the best, just the same as I am.

Tarrance Brooks

Hi, my name is Tarrance and I am a current student at Ballou Senior High School. I am an athlete and love sports. Sometimes I join programs like this to stay active and educated. In the future I would like to go to Miami University. Also I would love to become the most successful lawyer that ever lived. Ballou Story Project helped me better my writing skills and better my knowledge and I believe you should join, too! I hope to start a program of my own to inspire kids to dream big.

Photo: DaeDae Walker

I became a force
for power, resilience,
and speaking my own truth.

Butterfly
by Mecca Straughter

As a child I was an introvert. My timid personality always kept me from being social. I was raised by a single parent, and didn't have much family. My mother had to provide for me the best way she could, so that meant many nights her coming home late from work exhausted. I didn't have many friends. My hobbies were watching my hero Steve Erwin, the Crocodile Hunter, every day, and writing potential novels. I didn't speak much unless I was spoken to, but somehow when I was writing I had a lot to say. I was only seven whaen I wrote my first book. I wrote it on line paper and illustrated the whole book. My story was about the relationships between best friends. To this day I still have the book.

It was never easy being shy, but it got even harder in high school. Not only did I have to make new friends, but my mom was one of the assistant principals. My eleventh grade year was hard. I had gained many enemies unknowingly. It was through my mother that I had gained those enemies because of her disciplinary actions towards some students. I was tested by many. Through them I learned how much patience and endurance I had. I was aware of this and I didn't let them get the best of me. I sometimes wished I could be the 7-year-old me, and avoid them, but I knew that wasn't the answer.

One day my friend joined a new club and she brought me to the meeting with her because she was nervous. It was the Ballou Knights Poetry Club. I have written poetry before, but never thought it could actually be a serious hobby. I went in there with the intentions of being a source of support for my friend, but instead I became a part of the team. The only thing that scared me was showing and expressing my work to others. I was unsure of the reactions I would receive so I just took a chance, and let them hear my work. It was the best experience I've ever had.

When I joined I felt at home. All of my insecurities went out the window when I began writing. My voice was heard. They gave us prompts about self-worth. One exercise asked us to write a letter to someone begging them not to take something important from you, and I chose my name. My name is my identity. It was one of the first pieces I wrote.

My team was a slam team so we had to compete against others on stage. I had never competed before, and I became nervous. The day of our first competition, I was trying not to feel anything. My team and I watched other groups that had been performing for years, and we had just started practicing the month before. I was being forced to perform. I didn't want to. There was this one kid that performed before me. His energy took hold of the room. It felt as though we were in a trance. He stood 6'1, and he had an afro the size of his pride. His necklace was a black fist, which was held by a skinny black rope. It told me he knew his worth. He talked about black people ending violence against one another, and becoming unified. With one fist in the air he ended his poem with "love Jah Rastafari" (the founder of an African-based spiritual ideology). Then he exited the stage, and I was next to perform. Of course I would be after him.

"Mecca!" the lady called. I stood up and walked to the front with my team rooting for me. I stood in front of the mic and felt like my stomach dropped. All I wanted to do was leave the room, but my coach was standing in front of the door closest to me. So I spoke. I closed my eyes and began to recite. My poem was about my "roots," how I wanted to see where I came from. I opened my eyes to see the audience and the feeling of respect that I gained was unparalleled. Halfway into my poem I was still nervous but the words seem to roll off my tongue.

I want to search for my roots
…
Where women's noses and lips are pierced with wood
And men walk confident and tall, with skin dark as black diamonds

I was finished! All I could hear was a roar of applause. When I got back to my seat, the boy who performed before me said he never heard anything that great from a "rookie." I felt proud, and accomplished.

The slams gave me a boost of confidence in myself and in my writing. I was no longer timid, reserved or shy. The poetry club helped me find my voice; I was sort of an extrovert. I loved the new me.

I have always loved writing and now everyone had a chance to see my writing. Through poetry I became a published author. The book is called *The Weight of the Day Surrounds My Body*. It was a collaboration between DC high school students. I was one of few to have two poems of my own in the book.

I realized that I wasn't the only person overcoming my own obstacles of life. I have the ability to overcome anything. I became much more social, and I've gained great experiences when I finally spoke up and let my voice be heard. I adjusted the timid side of me and became a force for power, resilience, and speaking my own truth.

Mecca Straughter

I was born in Boston, MA and grew up in Washington, DC. I'm currently a 12th grader and will attend Tennessee State University in the fall. I want to continue poetry and to become a social activist.

Ways Band Helps You Realize the World

by Christopher Allen

The first day I showed up at practice for the Ballou marching band was in my ninth grade year. I was overwhelmed. We practiced down in the armory and there were a lot of people there. I knew a few people, but some I just met. I heard they were the number one band in the land, and that's why I joined.

That first day I walked in, I was scared to play. I didn't know people there well, and I didn't want them to laugh if I messed up. I chose to play the tuba because it's the biggest instrument in the band.

The first day of practice for me was calm, because all I learned was the scale. While they played songs I just stood there with my tuba on and watched. I tried to play but I couldn't. I would blow some notes and when I played, it came out, but it didn't sound right. I tried to play the right note but I couldn't hit it.

The next day I learned a song and I was ecstatic and it felt awesome. The first song I learned was "Turn Up the Music." It is hard to play because it has a lot of notes. It played in my head for days afterwards and it still does. I whistle the song in class and teachers get mad because it is irritating to them, but not me.

After one week I learned two songs and memorized them both because we played them over and over until the band director brought out a new song. We had to learn quickly because after only three weeks in the band we had a performance at Hampton to do their homecoming parade. It was fun and long at the same

Photo: DaSean Lee

If you have a dream,
and you're too afraid to do it,
just try.

time. Knowing how to play and march at the same time is hard to do. You have to have a lot of strength in your lungs and legs to not stop. It was hard, but it felt awesome performing for that first time. That's one reason why I stayed in the band: all the hard work and pain pays off. You know it, you get it, you just have to do it. And then comes the easy part: having fun.

The band director's name is Watson. He makes everyone around him laugh. He knows how to play every instrument in the band. He is a teacher, and he has a group called the WATsons, which stands for Willing Aspiring Teen sons. It's a mentor program that basically helps you stay focused on high school and your grades. He came up with the idea. He's a teacher so he doesn't want to see anyone fail.

Being in the band has a great responsibility. You have to keep your grades up, and everybody will be on you because you are in the band. Also, if you want to be the top high school band you have to practice. We practice almost three hours a day. You have to motivate yourself good. It's easy some of the time, but there is hard work getting ready to do a performance or a parade. You're practicing for a reason. You're practicing to remember and not to forget.

The other thing I've learned from band also applies to the rest of my life. Don't be shy if you can't hit the note. Just play so you can get help. If you're scared, just try. If you have a dream, and you're too afraid to do it, just try. If you fall, pick yourself back up. If you believe in something, you should try to make it feel right for you.

Christopher Allen

I was born in Washington, DC at an all-women's hospital. My name is Christopher Allen. I'm a ninth grade AVID student and a member of Ballou Story Project. I like to be in band and Reach. I like playing football, because it's Amercia's favorite pastime. So that's a little about me.

Long-Distance Mom
by N.C. Kitt

I was a teenage girl growing up without a mother on the daily. She moved away when I was twelve because my parents split up. My mother and I were like Bonnie and Clyde. She was always with me through anything. Any problems I had with my dad, she would help me. Dad and I used to argue weekly about simple things: leaving shoes around, food we both wanted, leaving my uniform on afterschool. If me and my dad had disagreements I would call my mom and my mom would tell me stories and reasons why things will get better.

My mom was a great mother. She had three children, and being a single mom, she did a lot. She sacrificed things for us, things she needed. She did what she had to do to pay the bills, like staying extra hours at work. We might not have had the most but we made it.

But then when I needed her most, she was gone.

I needed her as I grew up to become a lady. I needed her to show me how to deal with personal issues. I needed her to show me the way.

After my mom left I had nobody to tell my issues to. I felt like I didn't have a shoulder to cry on. It was hard. On Mondays when "Extreme Makeover: Home Edition" came on I had no one to watch it with. When I looked in the stands during basketball

Photo: DaSean Lee

I was a teenage girl
growing up without a mother
on the daily.

games, I had one less person cheering me on. Me and my dad grew apart. We didn't talk that much and I felt like he was the reason for my mom leaving. I felt like I couldn't tell him that because he wouldn't feel the same way. He would disagree. I had anger. How could he take the person I needed most in my life away?

This past summer, I decided the distance was too much for me to handle. I had a big argument with my dad and I just couldn't take it anymore. I couldn't start high school like this. So I called my mom and asked her, "Hey, by chance, can I come back home?"

I was holding onto the chair, hoping.

"You're always welcome," she said. I heard sniffles. "I've been missing you," she said.

So since then my mom is back in my life. Our connection is building stronger. With us being apart it kind of let us strengthen our relationship. I was sad at first, because over that time apart my mother did hurt me. But I knew I could look past that because of the bond that we had before.

A mother figure is a very important person in your life. She can share so many things with you that you can carry on for life. There are several girls I know who don't have the mother figure in their life that they should. Girls need that reflection from someone who has already gone through these things before. Someone who can be an example that things will get better, be the proof that nothing can hold you back.

When I get older I want to be a wonderful mother. I plan to share my experiences and mistakes with my children. I want to hold their hand while they cry, rub their back while they're going through their struggles. I will always motivate them to do what they believe in. I want to be a part of every moment of their life.

The time away from my mother taught me just how heartbroken you can feel from being away from the person you love the most. I will be that special someone that my kids can always come to.

N.C. Kitt

Hi. I'm N.C. Kitt and I'm 14. I live in Washington, DC. I have three sisters and one brother. I love to be social and go out and do outgoing things. In college I would like to major in psychology and biology to become a therapist and a pediatrician. Writing this piece was kind of difficult for me, but I knew it would help someone else with the same situation.

The Healer

by Dreonna Richardson

Ever since I was a little girl I have always aspired to help others. Out of my many siblings, my family always knew that I would be great. When my mother was cooking dinner, I was the one there washing the dishes. I was the one she trusted to watch my younger siblings when she went out. I used to read to them, and take them outside, or if they were hungry, I would feed them. I fulfilled the title of a true big sister from a young age.

I took my role as a mentor so seriously because others in my family didn't have that mindset. My mother was strong for as long as she could handle, but then she fell victim to drug addiction, and my family got split up. I realized that it would be hard for us, so I had to be strong and teach my siblings that even when your current or past circumstances aren't the best, you have the power to create a better future for yourself.

After my father took my two older siblings and I into custody, I was automatically put in the spotlight, because my older siblings were making poor decisions, trying to cope with the emptiness we felt without our mother. My father tried hard to teach us that education should be our main focus. However, I was the only one who internalized his wisdom, which led me to get good grades all throughout school. I would sacrifice playtime to do homework, or even read a book. Looking at my siblings I realized that someone had to be successful, and that someone would have to be me.

Around this time my grandmother, who was living with us, was diagnosed with schizophrenia. I had no clue what that was because I was so young. I couldn't even pronounce that word. It was a little funny at first, but then it got scary. All I knew was that

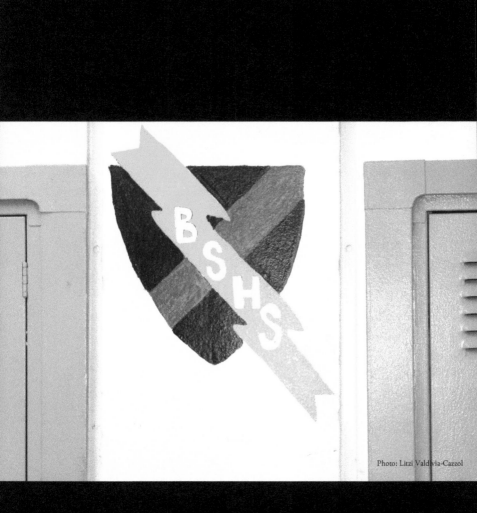

My purpose is to bring joy
to the lives of those who feel like
there is no joy.

she was yelling, and talking to herself, but I thought that was just her. My dad had a talk with me about the disease, and I became curious. How did this happen to people? And why? And what could be done about it?

My grandmother isn't the only one in my family with a mental disorder; there are some who have ADHD, bipolar disorder, and more, which further contributed to my interest. This was the beginning of my passion for not only wanting to learn about mental illness but also to combat people's perceptions of those who suffer from mental illness. I want them to feel normal, to not feel ashamed. Even when people do have something wrong with them, no one wants to be stuck in that black hole. Everyone wants to be happy. Nobody should be constantly reminded that they have this disease. It will only get worse if people are incessantly treating them like they're not capable of living a normal life.

I hope to study clinical psychology as my major so that I can fulfill what I believe to be my purpose: to bring joy to the lives of those who feel like there is no joy. Specifically, my calling is to help those with mental illness. College will enable me to pursue that goal by offering classes that help me learn more about mental health and by providing opportunities to intern and get hands-on experience. I have been through so much in my life, and I can honestly say I have been molded into a stronger individual. I know that college is that key to the door that I am determined to walk through. On the other side, I will be a mentor, and a healer, and I will dedicate my life to the happiness of those who need it most.

Dreonna Richardson

I am a very strong-willed person who always has intentions to succeed. I am from SE DC but I assure you that my character opposes the stereotypes of my city. I love laughing, playing my trumpet in the Ballou Majestic Marching Band, making people happy, and trying to be great at everything that I do. I am free-spirited and seen as a role model to many. I love life.

Journey of Becoming Me
by Randy Sams

I had to become the man of the house at a young age. When I was twelve, both of my older siblings went to jail. I'm not even sure why they went—maybe it was for gun possession or stealing a car or maybe even fighting. When I was with them, they never got in trouble. I was their younger brother so they never wanted me to get caught by the law. But when they were with their friends, trouble somehow found them. People they hung with were from a certain hood or gang. They would rob or might have even shot people. I grew up around the hood, so gangs were everywhere. But I was with kids my age around the block so I never really knew what type of trouble my brothers got into. And then one day they were gone.

The truth is I didn't want to grow up quickly. I had a history of trouble of my own. As a kid growing up I wasn't always the best behaving child. It started in elementary school when I used to act up and get suspended. I disrespected teachers and fought other classmates. I think I was trying to prove a point of where I stood. I wanted to be cool and popular to the kids at school. In fifth grade I threatened a teacher and got put out of school. I wasn't able to be a part of the fifth grade promotion and I got in big trouble. I even saw my mother cry.

Change started to come when I got to the sixth grade. I knew I had to change because I felt like I could do better for me and my mother. I didn't want her to be stressed with my behavior like she

Photo: DaSean Lee

To be a real man
it means to take charge
of your life.

was in the past, and like how she was stressed over my brothers. I wasn't perfect, and I still got in a little trouble, but my grades came way up.

I did even better in seventh grade. I got honor roll and a lot of rewards for my behavior and I barely got in trouble. All I did was make my mother proud that year and also made myself proud. This was especially important because this was the year that my brothers were gone. It was just me and my mother and I didn't want her having to be stressed. I wanted to be the one to make her proud.

A lot of things have made me change. My mother became sick and tired of my behavior. She tried to tell me how this behavior would get me put out of her house. She warned me that if my behavior kept on going the way it was I could be the third one to be behind bars, and this time she wouldn't be the one helping. She tried disciplining me but sometimes I still acted up. I didn't mean to, but if I did, I would just be thinking about myself.

Now my behavior is good. I'm busier with band, work, and my studies. What changed is how I was able to handle stuff. Now I think, I don't react like I used to. I used to get in more trouble, more fights, but when I learned to think first then I didn't get in trouble. Now I don't put myself in those situations or I just walk away.

What I want for myself in the future is to have my life organized. I want a healthy and strong relationship with my mother because without her I wouldn't be here. She made me the man I am and will be. To be a real man it means to take charge of your life. You provide and you help your household in any situation. You have to watch out and take care of people and if you don't do that, then you're not taking your responsibility serious. This is what I've learned, from watching my brothers grow up, and from overcoming my own obstacles. This is the promise I make to myself to get better in life.

Randy Sams

My name is Randy and I was born in Washington, DC on August 25, 1998. I am a student at Ballou Senior High School. I'm in the ninth grade. I write because it's a good way to express myself. I also write music and poetry. I can cook, and I'm a good dancer.

Photo: DaSean Lee

I never lose my faith in what I do,
even though people try
to put me down.

I keep on rising to the top.

Never Give Up (On Me)

by DaeDae Walker

On Saturdays when we had nothing else to do, my grandmother and I would just get up and go. We would go to the movies, downtown, or Old Navy. We would both get outfits for Sunday morning. Grandma really likes sweaters. We always listened to the radio, and she would laugh. Her laugh is so adorable. She tries to be loud but she can't get that loud. She's so small, like 5'1," I think.

I love everything about my grandma. She is fun to be with. She makes clothes and is an amazing cook, especially her homemade Mac & Cheese and Sweet Potato Pie. She loves kids and has been teaching for 33 years. She is also a Pastor and she can sing as well. And if you need help, she's always a good person to tell if you need prayer. She was the one everybody turned to.

When I was six years old my grandmother's life changed. On May 4, 2006 she went to work and got her annual mammogram. Within an hour she received a call from Radiology telling her that it was important that she returned to the X-Ray Department. She went back the next day, and they must have taken at least 26 images of her left breast. By the time they finished, she was instructed to see her primary physician. Soon after, Dr. Joshi informed her that there was lump in her breast, and it was cancer.

I don't remember being told that Grandma was sick. I don't remember when I learned what cancer was, or how hard it was to get through it. But now I know it was hard. Grandma had to get a lumpectomy, and then she was told she needed six months of chemo and 28 days of radiation. Radiation had to be the same time every day except Saturday and Sunday. After three months of chemo, her hair started to fall out.

It scared me when she was losing her hair. Before, every night she would roll her hair in little rows, and she combed it back so it would be curly. But then it started to fall out. It looked weird. It was like she had baby hair. Like how a newborn baby's hair is so soft and silky. And she was always in the hospital, too. We went to visit her and I always cried because I didn't want to leave her there. People die in hospitals. If I lost my grandmother, it would have been like I lost everything.

I would pray for her and help her with things, but every morning my grandmother would get up and make breakfast and go to work like there was nothing wrong at all. She would always keep a smile on her face. She never had her head down, and she went to work like nothing was wrong. She was very strong.

But we did not know if she was going to make it. That was the scary part.

When it was time for radiation, the trip every day was tiresome. Thankfully she had an excellent team of doctors who also became her friends. She thanks God for the knowledge he gave to them.

Finally, after the 28 long days, she made it through. Thank the Lord. She was prescribed medication for the next five years, though. It was rough. The real victory came in August of 2013. After her mammogram her surgeon and friend Dr. Sallie Davis told her that she no longer needed to see her. She is now what they called "History." Hallelujah!

For us all my grandmother is an amazing, strong, and brave woman. Nobody wanted to lose her at all. My life would be hard without her even though sometimes I don't do good by her when I should, but it's getting better. I try to follow her lesson, but sometimes I get tired of fighting and I give up. But like her, I never lose my faith in what I do, even though people try to put me down. I keep on rising to the top.

I have learned that no matter where life takes you, always keep your head up. Grandma taught me the most important lesson: never give up on God because he won't give up on you, and always have faith in yourself even when nobody else does. At the end of the day you notice you came into this world alone and that's the way you're going out. Grandma taught me that. No matter what I go through, I will never give up on myself.

DaeDae Walker

I grew up in SE DC around Wahler. I've been with my grandmother since I was five. I like to draw and write in my free time. My birthday is October 9th.

Without My Father

by DaSean Lee

I was born fourteen days before Christmas, on my father's birthday. He wasn't there when I was born because he was at the club. I was supposed to be born a day later. He dropped my mother off at the hospital and then he went to the club. He came back afterwards, but I think she was upset. After I came to this earth, though, she was in a good mood because I was her first child.

I barely remember anything about him. When I was two, my father was killed. He was killed because he didn't want to give up something he had. He was drinking behind the house in an alley with his friends. One of his friends tried to rob him, and they started getting into it. Then that person left and came back, and he came with a weapon. My mother was the one who heard the gunshot. She looked outside and she asked where our father was, and her neighbor told her. She saw the whole thing.

People are always telling me how I look like my father, the way he used to be. They say that my hair, my nose, my skin color are all the same. I hear it from his old friends, our family members, but I never got to see it myself. They say even our actions are the same. For example, they say he was goofy, playful, like to joan on people. My mother told me that when I was little me and my father went to the 7-11 and got a chili hot dog and she said we came back with chili all over me. He sounds like he was a lot of fun. He sounds like someone I would have liked to have around.

I wonder how my life would be different if my father was here. Even though my father passed, he's still doing better than many fathers who are here, because we do get retirement money every

Photo: Randy Sams

I will be the father
that I wish I had.

month from his job. But honestly his death is still too much pressure on my mom. She has to pay for everything we have, like clothing, shoes, food. But if my father was living they would go 50/50 on everything.

Not many of my friends have a father in their household either. They tell me things like their father was supposed to do something he didn't do, and their mother has to do it for them. Things like their fathers not paying for nothing or caring. It seems like no father seems to care about settling down and taking care of their kids. Nobody my age even knows the definition of a lifelong relationship.

This means there are going to be a lot of single parents in my generation. They're making babies and they don't have a place to live. They don't have jobs. When their father isn't there, they're taking after him, doing as he did. You know your mother taught you better as a single parent, so that's what you do.

I won't do that to my child. The women in my life won't have to worry about me leaving or not paying for anything. I will always be in my child's life. As a father I will give my child the things she needs and wants. I will finish school, go to college, and finish with a degree. I will go out in the real world and get a job. Then I will settle down, have a kid, maybe get married. I won't ever be out of my child's life. I see myself at nighttime reading her a bedtime story, taking him to the movies. I will be swimming with him in the swimming pool. Going to the mall. Racing go-carts.

I will be the father that I wish I had.

DaSean Lee

My name is DaSean Lee and I go to Ballou Senior High School. I'm in the 9th grade in AVID, taking all honors classes. I am a very athletic person and I like to play sports. I wish my father was here so my mother wouldn't go through the things she does but also because I miss him.

Creating a Change

by Charles'e Thornton

I am the ninth of eleven children, and we grew up in an area of difficulty and violence. Most nights I was awakened by gunshots or sirens. I was reluctant to watch the news because I knew that it was nothing but the same stories, only different circumstances. At times my house was the target of the gunfire. This was due to most of family running the streets or in jail gaining enemies. This was very stressful because at times I wasn't able to go outside, sometimes even school, in fear of my safety. I grew tired of looking over my shoulders from troubles that had nothing to do with me. I decided that I had to get away and create a safer living environment.

We also moved around a lot. Throughout my middle and high school years, I was transient. I switched back and forth between schools in Washington, DC and Greensboro, NC seven or eight times. There was even a point where my family and I had nowhere to go and moved into a motel. This caused a really low state of self-esteem. My parents weren't able to provide the way other parents could. This situation also made them feel down. Their sadness caused a decline in both of their health. Seeing my parents this way added to the depression.

Moving to new places can tough because you are constantly trying to catch up on school subjects. I was beginning to stray from education and lean towards the life that many of my family members have taken. I started skipping school and doing other things that didn't live up to my values.

I'm determined
to create a change
in my community.

During my last move back to DC, I knew I had to make a change if I was going to be successful. I moved in with my grandmother, and she always stressed the importance of education. I looked at my transcript one day and knew I had to do better. I began to pay attention in school and earn the grades that I knew were up to my capability. I attended school on a regular basis and stayed focused on my future. I realized I wanted more out of life. I want to be independent, self-sufficient, and able to provide for myself. I don't want to lose these qualities despite the many challenges that I have already faced and that I may face in the future.

Now I try to use my experiences to become better and never drift to that state of mind again. Though this was a tough period in life for a minor, I have gained a great amount of strength and knowledge. I learned to appreciate the things that are in front of you. I also learned that one of the only things that can't be taken from you is your knowledge. This great thing can take you far or hold you back, depending on how it is used.

Getting a college education is important to me for various reasons. Considering I will be the first in my family to go to college, I would like to set an example for my two younger siblings. I want them to know that with hard work, anything is possible. I'm determined to create a change in my community. I plan to study criminal justice and psychology so that I can learn about the roots of the problems that I have faced at such a young age and help develop plans to keep youth from experiencing the things that I have. That's my inspiration. That's my future.

Charles'e Thornton

Writing this essay was a challenge for me. I never expressed my experience with people. I feel that this piece has helped me to release some mental tensions I have faced.

Becoming a Young Adult

by Gerald McBrayer, III

The first time I rode the bus by myself, I was about twelve years old, and I was nervous. I just wanted to see how it felt to get on the bus by myself. I was going all the way on Benning Road to go over to my aunt's house, on the W4. It would take me an hour to get all the way over there.

When I told my mom, she was surprised. She thought I was too young, and she didn't know that I wanted to get on the bus by myself. But I felt like I could do it. I was getting older, and I wanted to prove to her that I was responsible enough to get on the bus on my own. When I left, she said, "Be careful," and told me to call her when I reached my destination.

I left the house feeling brave, but on my way there, I got nervous. When I was riding the bus with my mom, we'd get off at the stop in front of the gas station, so I knew that was my stop. But I was worried that I wasn't going to see it. I thought that I was going to get off at the wrong stop. I thought that I wasn't going to make it there.

When the bus pulled up I knew it was time. I got on, and it was crowded and I had to stand up. The people on the bus were loud, babies were crying, and it was a lot of commotion. It also was hot. It was about 92 degrees outside. The bus was very cold because the bus driver had turned the air conditioner on.

It was so crowded I didn't know if I would be able to ring the bell. At one point I got to sit down, but then an old lady got on the bus so I got up and let her sit in my seat. I had to stand up for the rest of the ride.

It's also good to grow up.
It makes you feel
release.

Finally, my stop came, and I got off. A lot of other people got off, too. It wasn't as hard as I thought it was.

When I reached my destination, I had to walk up a hill to get to my aunt's house. When I got to my aunt's house, she asked me, "How did you get over here?" I told her that I got on the bus by myself and she said, "Really?" I said, "Yes."

This was the first time I actually did something on my own, like an adult. It was the first of many. Now I walk to far places on my own, cook for myself, take care of my nieces and nephews. I've had to move around a lot, from Northeast DC to Southeast DC and house to house. I've had to deal with sad things that encouraged me to become a young adult. So many other family members and friends have had to deal with the same things that I've dealt with.

It's hard to grow up. It can be terrifying. I'm going to have to deal with consequences of what I do, and that's a lot of responsibility. I have to make sure that I don't get into any trouble. But it's also good to grow up. It makes you feel release. I'm released from people treating me like a little kid, not taking me seriously. I'm mature now, I'm growing up. I have plans for myself. I want to go to college and graduate. I want to become famous playing football or study hard to become a doctor. I want to take care of my mom as she gets older. I want to have a family. And I want to help my kids go through this same scary, joyful, liberating process of becoming an adult.

Gerald McBrayer, III

My name is Gerald McBrayer. I am a current student at Ballou Senior High School. I am fifteen years old. I have four siblings, three nieces, and two nephews. I live with a single parent in a house full of joy. I love to play sports. I was born in Washington, DC.

Anything Is Possible
by Nadiya Holley

While many people look to receive money the fast way, I choose to do what's best for me. I've always had this mentality that going to college is imperative. Although neither of my parents went to college, they have worked hard and provided for me. They supported me through the years by making sure that I didn't need or want for anything. They want the best for me, so they stay on me about homework and school. They're good parents, but I know they could have more opportunities with a college education. So therefore I aspire to attend college and show appreciation to my parents for all their hard work.

I want to go to college because I have big goals in life. I've always been a dedicated athlete, and I have real dreams of playing in the WNBA. But that's not my only goal: I also want to be an orthopedic in sports medicine. Some people who go to the WNBA don't finish college because they accept offers to play professionally before receiving a degree. They won't have anything to fall back on if something bad happens. If they get injured or if it doesn't work out how they expected, they need to have other options. I prefer to get my degree so I can have success after a basketball career. I'm prepared to work harder in college so that I can pursue my dreams.

It hasn't always been easy. Because where I come from isn't a gated community or suburbs, I've always had to deal with non-believers. People in and out of my community think we're not

Photo: Nina Kitt

My future is too bright
to allow someone else's thoughts to
bring me down.

capable of anything because of where we reside. They try to bring you down by saying things like "You're never going to be this or that because of where you were raised" or "You don't know how to do this like the kids in private schools." Throughout this situation I've learned to prove non-believers wrong by having a tenacious attitude. I worked hard through the situation by allowing myself to maintain a high GPA, taking mostly AP courses, and being involved with many activities. I stay after school and lunch to get extra help from teachers. I also play many sports like basketball, flag football, softball, and volleyball. As captain of the basketball team I have developed my leadership skills and my ability to lead by example.

I do these things not only to prove others wrong, but to make my life worthy. I use people's negative thoughts as motivation, which is a bonus to my success. To block all the negative attention most black people receive, I just stand out and do my best at whatever I do. These types of experiences influence my day-to-day life by pushing me harder. Knowing I have people who don't believe in me makes me an even better person. My future is too bright to allow someone else's thoughts to bring me down. So therefore I'm going to continue doing what I do, and I will prove to them that anything is possible.

Nadiya Holley

I grew up in SE DC. I like to shop and I like music, like R&B and rap. My favorite artist is Lightshow. I'm going to Marshall University and will play basketball for them. I like telling people what I want to be in life and what I'm going to do to accomplish my goals.

How to Grow Up Like Me
by M.S. Holiday

1. Be born.

I was born in October. Before me was my older brother, and before him was my other brother watching over me. That brother I never knew. He didn't make it. I almost didn't make it, too.

As a baby, I got a real bad fever. I cried and you could feel the warmth on my skin. My mother held me. They called a doctor and he put me in a bucket of ice, or so Mom said. I shivered and squirmed. This happened far away where it was expensive to even call a doctor. But they called him, and he said that if I survived something like this, I would either be very intelligent or have mental problems. My family was worried.

After some time, the fever broke. And now I'm here, telling my story.

2. Remember your beginnings.

When I was a baby we moved in with a lot of different family members since my parents were unemployed at the time. We stayed at relatives' houses even though my parents talked bad about them and most of them had a criminal record.

I tried to enjoy my childhood. I tried to avoid the bad stuff. I was always hanging out with my cousin Sarah who played with my hair, watched over me, made me laugh. I didn't hang out with my older cousins who were always partying and didn't want to watch over me. My aunt Sue loved to cook, but she always started a conflict in the family because of gossip. I wish I lived with them, but I understood that I could not. I felt like I was homeless at this time, renting a living room in a townhouse, living with my grandma and grandpa, who were good to me. My grandmother cooked and my grandfather worked at a grocery store. When he came back from work, he always had a treat.

3. Be a kid.

I was a good kid and always did my best. But my parents were always pushing me to do better, which is good. Encouragement is good. I just think that maybe if they could stop and tell me to be a kid, have sleepovers, hang out with friends, have a birthday party, that would've been a nicer encouragement. Once I realized that wasn't likely to happen I stopped and changed, but I had my reasons.

4. Change for a reason.

When you change you always have a reason, even if it's a dumb one.

I was really quiet when I was little, and I moved around a lot. I didn't want to make friends because I didn't want to get close and lose them. It was kind of like a cycle: I went to school and I went home and I didn't really go outside. I needed a reason to keep on going, to not give up. School was the only way out, the only way to escape.

When I was at school I tried to distract myself from what was happening, or what could be happening, at home.

I used to like school, but then I stopped caring. I got good grades but that wasn't important. I didn't really have anything important at the time. I stopped caring about everything. I'd numb down my feelings, like a robot. I thought if I could ignore what was happening, it wasn't really happening.

5. Adapt to the environment.

At first it was just my mother. But then it got to be me and my brothers, too, because we tried to break it up. But we were little and he was too big. He would push us to the side and beat us up and then go back to beating up my mother. She would take it, because she knew if she didn't or if she tried to fight back he would hurt us more.

6. Don't overthink.

When I was a kid it was the best time because I didn't overthink. I didn't overthink about the pain physically because I thought emotionally and mentally that I was okay. I thought when people said, "Love hurts," I should be proud, because at the moment I had the best love. My father beat on me, and I thought that was love.

The only love I came across at the time.

7. Face your fears.

I tried to run away.

The police put me in the back of their car with no handles and they took me home to my abusive father and helpless mother who couldn't leave because there was not enough money. Then the officer told me he would lock me up if I ran away again.

Photo: DaSean Lee

We are all children who don't know
what's happening but all want
desperately to survive.

8. Be quiet.

I learned how people acted or code switched when around other people, like my parents around me, and then my parents around my social worker. For example at home around my social worker I'm my best self, that's what my dad taught me, but that wasn't so different, because I don't beat up people when the social worker isn't around.

9. Don't.

Don't trust. My mom took my Dad's side even if she had bruises from last night to prove just how "lucky" she was. I thought I could trust them because their DNA created me, but I had to think twice because when I was helping my mom, it was her and my dad that brought me down.

Don't snitch. After I got tired of abuse I didn't say anything or else my mother would curse me out and neglect me because I tried to stop her from getting bruised up so much and she's started to get short tempers.

Don't cry. Tears don't help. I've tried many times.

Don't let what they do affect you even though it has. Don't let it show.

10. Try to understand your mom.

I felt like my mother told me that she loved me and never meant it, because when she did I felt like she didn't mean it, or it didn't feel like a mother-to-daughter love. She would say it for like five seconds and then change back to being distant. It looked like she would be at a different place when she said it, and then she'd come back. She didn't normally show her emotions.

She got close and then she went away.

11. Get good grades.

It's the only chance I have to run away from this life. I like to do my homework in the living room next to my mom so I can have a better chance of making sure she's okay. I like English because it's the only thing that lets me say what I want.

12. Believe.

Knowledge and faith is what kept me going when I felt like I was alone, and when I was alone. People say to follow your heart but I didn't want any emotions wrapped up with what was already happening, so I just had my knowledge. My faith has always been with me. Without it, I would not be here writing this.

13. Let time pass.

...

...

...

14. Move on.

I started from mostly crying myself to sleep, or sleeping with everything deep inside me. Yeah, you can hold it in, but your heart might not have space for it, or your mind. I'm not saying cry yourself to sleep every night but I'm saying move on. Learn that there's no such thing as a yellow brick road if you're lost. So find yourself because you can't understand anything if you don't understand yourself.

I learned that a while ago and I'm still trying to find myself, but I've been doing fine, I've tied up a few loose ends, and have been happy lately. No, not the fake-plastic-mask-happy but happy because I don't have much pain left. I'm moving on. I'm a good student who's smart and has a lot going for her. My relationship between me and my mother hasn't been perfect but it's better. As for my father, after a year or two of having a social worker, he's changed. Maybe for the better, but only he knows that. He's still my father. He's not the best but not the worst. I've slowly forgiven him but not all the way. We've been working on it, saying hi, having a conversation here and there. It's better than before. We can be inside the same room without arguing, so that's something.

15. Get over it.

You'll turn crazy if you don't. If you do, you'll be crazy still but won't die while being alive.

16. Dream.

That older brother who is watching over me from heaven, he's also letting me know life is short and I should do my best to make my dreams come true.

My dream is to be a social worker since I know what it's like to want one. Someone who can understand the path that a child goes down because it is like the path I traveled.

I want to be the one who someone would want.

17. Grow up.

Someone has hurt you. Maybe not physically, but someone has and it broke you. I understand that, I really do, but you can't stay broken. Being broken shows weakness and it's a cold world out there where the weak don't survive. I didn't like that lesson. I didn't like anything or anyone because of something someone did, so I had to grow up. I had to be strong and so do you. We can do it together.

I was a baby when the fever came. I didn't understand what was happening but I survived with the bucket of ice. Let this story be your ice. Shock alive or another heartbeat for you since your heart has gone on mute. We are all children who don't know what's happening but all want desperately to survive.

M.S. Holiday

I wasn't born in DC but I might as well have been. I'm not the only child in my family. I like to sleep, eat, and I'm terrible at sports. I like to help people, though. That's what I want to do: help people who don't get help.

Note to Readers: Please know that this writer is now safe and that all precautions have been taken to maintain her safety. We commend her honesty and courage in sharing her story.

Acknowledgments

The Ballou Story Project could not have been possible without the dedication and support of a number of hard-working folks who believed in the importance of empowering these young people to write and share their stories.

For the striking photography throughout this book we thank Shout Mouse Photo Coach and ShootBack founder Lana Wong. Lana brought her considerable artistic talent to these writers and in a single afternoon coached them to create the beautiful images we see here. We are grateful for her dedication and her vision.

For coordinating the ninth grade AVID writers every week, we cannot thank enough Ballou teacher Shajena Erazo. Ms. Erazo was the motivating force behind these authors, and she gave selflessly of her time over and over again to make this project happen. She is an inspiration to her students and to those of us at Shout Mouse Press, and we are grateful for her support!

For coordinating the senior writers, we appreciate the time and energy of senior guidance counselor Kira Rowe. Ms. Rowe recruited and rallied these writers despite a very busy schedule supporting the senior class. She plays a tremendous role in the lives of her students and we thank her for making it possible for them to become authors.

We are grateful to Principal Rahman Branch for allowing us to come into Ballou to work with these students, and to Melissa Jackson, the library media specialist, for graciously hosting workshops and revision sessions in the iLab and Media Center.

None of this work would have been possible without a generous grant from the HMFC fund, for which we are incredibly grateful. The folks behind this fund introduced us to Ballou and served as constant encouragement and support.

And most of all we thank these seventeen dedicated writers who voluntarily gave up lunch periods and stayed after school and worked on pieces from home, always driven by the power of sharing their story with readers who needed to hear it. The selflessness and courage and tremendous strength of these authors will stay with us. We are so proud. Writing with—and learning from—these incredible teens was such a gift, and a joy.

About Shootback

Shootback empowers young people to tell their own stories and express their creative voices through photography, writing, and critical thinking about the world around them. Shootback started in Nairobi, Kenya in 1997 by putting cameras in the hands of teens from Mathare, one of Africa's largest slums, and culminated in the publication of *Shootback: Photos by Kids from the Nairobi Slums,* a documentary film, and an international traveling exhibition. Seventeen years on, Shootback continues to train a new generation of young photographers and now runs after-school programming in DC public schools in collaboration with various nonprofit organizations.

Shout Mouse Press is proud to partner with the Shootback team, who coach our authors to produce striking original photography for our books.

SHOOTBACK   www.ShootbackProject.org

73

About Shout Mouse Press

Shout Mouse Press is a writing program and publishing house for unheard voices. We partner with other nonprofit organizations serving communities in need and design custom book projects that benefit their communities. Our mission is two-fold:

- To amplify the voices of marginalized communities by empowering them to write and publish their stories.
- To amplify the missions of the nonprofits with whom we partner by creating tangible, marketable products that diversify and innovate their outreach and fundraising.

Shout Mouse Press was founded in Washington, DC in 2014. Our authors have produced original children's books, memoir collections, and novels-in-stories that engage readers of all literacy levels, ages, and backgrounds. See our full catalog of books on our website.

www.ShoutMousePress.org

We Believe

We believe everyone has a story to tell. We believe everyone has the ability to tell it. We believe by listening to the stories we tell each other—whether true or imagined, of hopes or heartbreaks or fantasies or fears—we are learning empathy, diplomacy, reflection, and grace. We believe we need to see ourselves in the stories we are surrounded by. We believe this is especially true for those who are made to believe that their stories do not matter: the poor or the sick or the marginalized or the battered. We feel lucky to be able to help unearth these stories, and we are passionate about sharing these unheard voices with the world.

SHOUT**MOUSE**
PRESS

CPSIA information can be obtained
at www.ICGtesting.com
Printed in the USA
LVHW07s0951130418
573253LV00029B/325/P